An Imprint of Pop!
popbooksonline.com

Desserts from Around the World

CAKES FROM AROUND THE WORLD

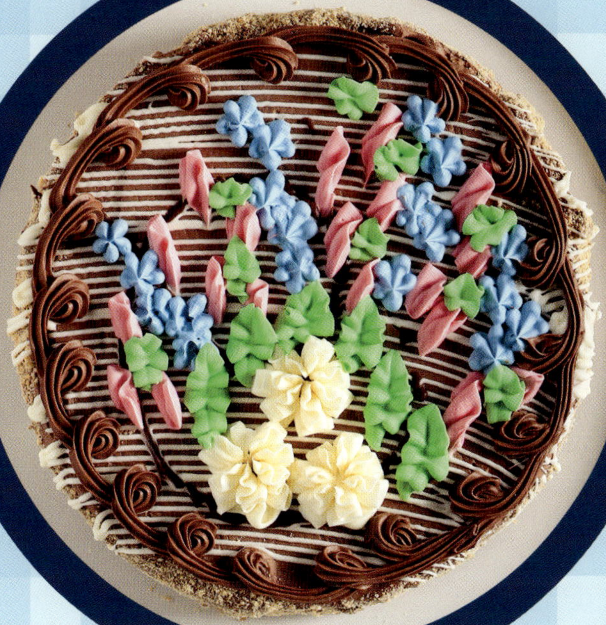

by Grace Hansen

WELCOME TO DiscoverRoo!

This book is filled with videos, puzzles, games, and more! Scan the QR codes* while you read, or visit the website below to make this book pop.

popbooksonline.com/cake

abdobooks.com

Published by Pop!, a division of ABDO, PO Box 398166, Minneapolis, Minnesota 55439.

Printed in the United States of America, North Mankato, Minnesota.

102024
012025

Cover Photo: Shutterstock Images
Interior Photos: Shutterstock Images, Getty Images
Editor: Elizabeth Andrews
Series Designer: Laura Graphenteen

Library of Congress Control Number: 2024938597

Publisher's Cataloging-in-Publication Data

Names: Hansen, Grace, author.
Title: Cakes from around the world / by Grace Hansen
Description: Minneapolis, Minnesota : Pop!, 2025 | Series: Desserts from around the world | Includes online resources and index
Identifiers: ISBN 9781098247096 (lib. bdg.) | ISBN 9781098247652 (ebook)
Subjects: LCSH: Baking--Juvenile literature. | Desserts--Juvenile literature. | Baked products --Juvenile literature. | Cakes--Juvenile literature. | Confectionery--Juvenile literature. | Cookery--Juvenile literature.
Classification: DDC 641.8653--dc23

*Scanning QR codes requires a web-enabled smart device with a QR code reader app and a camera.

TABLE OF CONTENTS

CHAPTER 1

THE HISTORY OF DESSERT

Desserts can be traced back to ancient times. The Mesopotamians had a fruitcake-like recipe. The Ancient Egyptians sweetened round, flat breads with dates and honey and cooked them over hot stones.

Much of what we know about the Ancient Egyptians comes from wall paintings in temples and tombs.

The shape celebrated the sun and moon. The Ancient Romans enjoyed simple sweet treats such as fruits, honey cakes, and fruit tarts.

This English oil painting from 1867 shows a first birthday celebration with cake and a candle.

In the 7th century, Persia (now Iran) was one of the first to harvest sugar cane and make cake-like cookies. In the 1500s, sugar became more affordable and widely available. In 1596, a cookbook was published for the growing middle classes in England. In it was a recipe for Fine Cakes. Later, Europeans made it more common to serve dessert, especially cake, for special occasions such as weddings.

Between 800 and 900, the Persians brought sugar cane to Southern Europe.

To this day, desserts help people around the world start the day, complete a meal, and celebrate important **milestones** and holidays. Let's go around the world and learn about cakes from different places and **cultures**!

Almond cake, such as the one in this Ancient Roman mosaic, would have required a great amount of effort to prepare.

Mochi has long been enjoyed in Japan to celebrate the New Year. It was said to harden the teeth and therefore extend life.

CHAPTER 2

CAKES FROM EUROPE

The Europeans make cakes fit for royals! The Victoria Sponge was named after Queen Victoria of England. It is said that she enjoyed this treat with her afternoon tea. The recipe calls for simple ingredients, such as flour, sugar, eggs,

LEARN MORE HERE!

and butter. Strawberry jelly is sandwiched between two light sponge cakes. The cake is not iced. Rather, it is finished with a light dusting of powdered sugar.

Queen Victoria's dinners could last up to three hours. For the final course, many desserts, such as cakes and ice cream bombes, were presented.

DID YOU KNOW?

Today's Princess Cake recipes often call for layers of jam or raspberries. The original recipe did not include fruit.

Princess Cake is a traditional Swedish dessert. It consists of alternating layers of sponge cake and pastry cream. A dome of whipped cream sits on top. It is finished with a green **marzipan** overlay and sprinkled with powdered sugar. The recipe was created in the late 1920s by Jenny Åkerström in honor of Sweden's three princesses at the time.

BLACK FOREST CAKE

Black Forest Cake is a classic German dessert. Its main ingredients include chocolate cake, cherries, and whipped cream. The Black Forest is an area in southwestern Germany known for its thick forests and lovely villages. It is said that an early form of the dessert came from this region.

Roll Cake is known by many names, including Swiss roll and jelly roll. Where Roll Cake originated is still up for debate. Some credit Central Europe while others credit North America. In any case, it remains a popular dessert throughout the world. Roll Cake is made by carefully rolling warm sponge cake. However, it can't be so warm that it melts the delicious whipped cream, jam, or buttercream filling!

Roll Cakes come in all sorts of colors and flavors.

DID YOU KNOW?

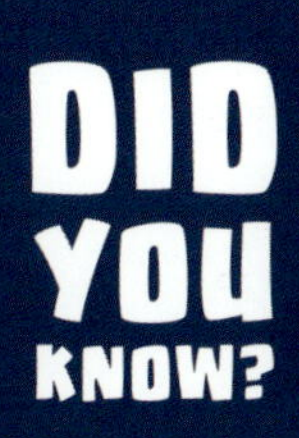

Roll Cake is popular to serve with afternoon tea in England. In France, Yule Log Cakes are popular around Christmastime.

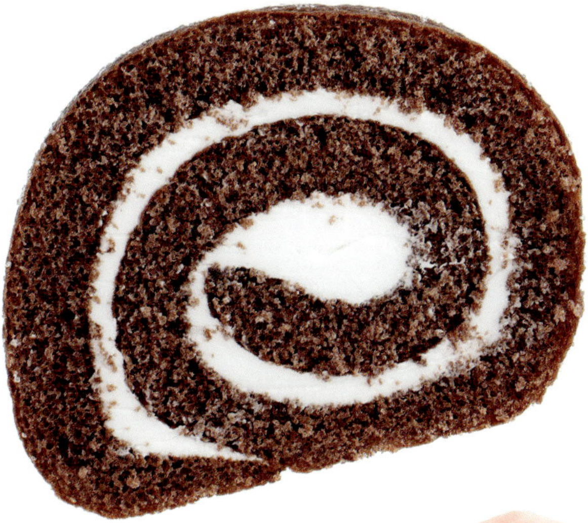

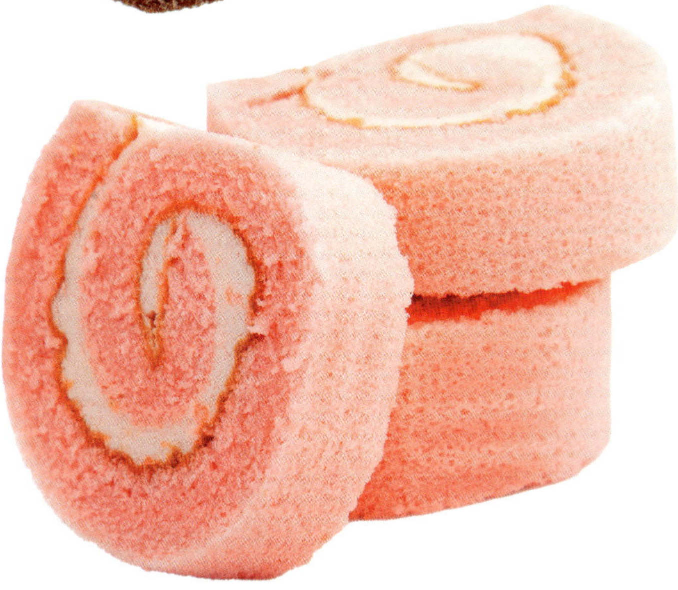

CHAPTER 3

CAKES FROM THE AMERICAS

The United States lays claim to the creation of some of the most decadent cakes, including Red Velvet Cake, Coconut Cake, and New York Cheesecake. The cocoa in Red Velvet Cake helps break down the flour's texture. This is what makes the cake so velvety soft.

EXPLORE LINKS HERE!

The Waldorf-Astoria hotel in New York City famously began serving Red Velvet Cake in the 1930s.

The shredded coconut can be raw or toasted.

Coconut Cake is a delicious white layer cake covered in coconut buttercream and shredded coconut. It has its origins in the American South. The first Coconut Cakes in America were crafted by people who were enslaved. It was Black women from Africa who knew how to break down the tough coconut fruit into something **divine**.

SWEETS FOR CIVIL RIGHTS

A group of women in Montgomery, Alabama, came together to support the Montgomery bus **boycotts** (1955-1956). They raised money by baking and selling sweet treats. Some of their most popular items were sweet potato pies and coconut layer cakes.

Though cheesecake has delighted people for centuries, New York Cheesecake has only been around since 1929. This is when restaurant owner Arnold Reuben replaced the cottage cheese in traditional recipes with cream cheese.

New York Cheesecake flavors are endless!

Cheesecakes adorn bakery displays throughout New York.

Cake baker Sonia Fernandez pours milk onto a Tres Leches Cake in a bakery in San Francisco, California.

Soaked cakes have been a **delicacy** for years. But none are as famous as Latin America's Tres Leches Cake. The dessert got its name for the three different milks used in it: evaporated milk, condensed milk, and cream. Air bubbles form in the process of baking the very light cake. This keeps it from becoming soggy despite being soaked.

Tres Leches Cake is often topped with whipped cream and cinnamon or fruit.

CHAPTER 4

CAKES FROM ASIA AND THE MIDDLE EAST

Mochi is not cake in the traditional sense. It is a Japanese rice cake. Though it is eaten year-round, it is most often made to celebrate the Japanese New Year. Traditionally, Mochi is made by using a wooden mallet to **pulverize** rice that has

COMPLETE AN ACTIVITY HERE!

Traditional Mochi making can be exciting to watch!

been soaked overnight and steamed. Simpler preparation involves whisking together a sweetened rice flour with liquid and cooking it in the microwave or on a stovetop.

Basbousa is a sweet semolina cake that dates back to the **Ottoman Empire**. It later became a popular dessert in Egypt. It is known by several different names, such as *revani* and *harisseh*, and comes in different variations throughout

Vegan Basbousa recipes call for apple sauce to replace the dairy and eggs.

DID YOU KNOW?

Muslims often eat Basbousa during Ramadan and Eid. Christians use the cake to celebrate the end of Lent.

Arabic-speaking people may call their loved ones "basbousa," which means something like "my sweetie."

the Middle East and North Africa. The Egyptian recipe calls for coconut and drenching the cake in syrup. Each slice is decorated with almonds.

MORE CAKES FROM AROUND THE WORLD!

1. Chocotorta (Argentina)
2. Meskouta (Morocco)
3. Dundee Cake (Scotland)
4. Kyiv Cake (Ukraine)
5. Mawa Cake (India)
6. Sans Rival (Philippines)
7. Pavlova (Australia and New Zealand)

Countries and **cultures** around the world have their own unique and traditional desserts. Their ingredients and techniques can be similar to or very different from one another.

MAKING CONNECTIONS

TEXT-TO-SELF

Do you like cake? If so, what is your favorite kind?

TEXT-TO-TEXT

Have you read any other books about food from around the world? What did you learn from those books that was not in this one?

TEXT-TO-WORLD

What are some other ways, besides dessert, that countries and cultures from around the world are special and different from one another?

GLOSSARY

boycott — to refuse to buy, use, or go to, in order to make a protest or bring about a change.

culture — the language, customs, ideas, and art of a particular group of people.

delicacy — something delightful or rare, especially food.

divine — excellent or delightful.

marzipan — a sweet paste made of almonds, egg whites, and sugar, and often molded into decorative forms.

milestone — an important event or turning point in history or in a person's life.

Ottoman Empire — also known as the Turkish Empire, an imperial realm that spanned much of Southeast Europe, West Asia, and North Africa from the 14th to early 20th centuries.

pulverize — to make into powder, as by crushing, grinding, or pounding.

INDEX

DiscoverRoo!
ONLINE RESOURCES

This book is filled with videos, puzzles, games, and more! Scan the QR codes* while you read, or visit the website below to make this book pop.

popbooksonline.com/cake

*Scanning QR codes requires a web-enabled smart device with a QR code reader app and a camera.